My First Picture Encyclopedia

A+ books

Show Me
SPACE

by Steve Kortenkamp

CAPSTONE PRESS
a capstone imprint

A+ Books are published by Capstone Press,
1710 Roe Crest Drive, North Mankato, Minnesota 56003.
www.capstonepub.com

Library of Congress Cataloging-in-Publication Data
Kortenkamp, Steve.
 Show me space : my first picture encyclopedia / by Steve Kortenkamp.
    p. cm.—(A+ books. My first picture encyclopedias)
 Summary: "Defines through text and photos core terms related to space"
       —Provided by publisher.
 ISBN 978-1-62065-058-5 (library binding)
 ISBN 978-1-62065-922-9 (paper over board)
 ISBN 978-1-4765-1345-4 (ebook PDF)
 1. Outer space—Exploration—Juvenile literature. I. Title. II. Series: My first picture
       encyclopedias.
  QB500.22.K577 2013
  520.3—dc23   2012026447

Editorial Credits
Christopher L. Harbo, editor; Bobbie Nuytten, designer; Svetlana Zhurkin, media
researcher; Laura Manthe, production specialist

Photo Credits
CDC: Janice Haney Carr, 11 (top right); Digital Vision, 9 (middle right), 22 (left and top right), 23 (middle left); Dreamstime: Aiyoshi, 12, Kenneth Sponsler (telescope),
cover, 30 (bottom left); ESA: C. Carreau, 31 (bottom), NASA/JPL-Caltech/STScI, 29 (middle right); ESO: L. Calçada and N. Risinger, 17 (top right), M. Kornmesser/L.
Calçada, 18 (top right); International Astronomical Union, 17 (middle left); iStockphotos: Rob Sylvan, 30 (top left); NASA, cover (astronaut and rover), back cover (middle
left), 1 (top right), 2 (bottom), 13 (top right), 17 (bottom), 21 (top), 24 (middle left), 30 (top right), 31 (top and middle right), Andrew S. Wilson (University of Maryland)/
Patrick L. Shopbell (Caltech)/Chris Simpson (Subaru Telescope)/Thaisa Storchi-Bergmann and F. K. B. Barbosa (UFRGS, Brazil)/Martin J. Ward (University of Leicester,
U.K.), 29 (middle), CXC/Eureka Scientific/M. Roberts et al., 25 (top middle), CXC/IfA/D. Sanders et al. (x-ray)/STScI/NRAO/A. Evans et al. (optical), 28 (left), CXC/SAO/F.
Seward et al., 25 (top right), ESA/H. Weaver (JHUAPL)/A. Stern (SwRI)/The HST Pluto Companion Search Team, 22 (bottom right), ESA/J. Hester and A. Loll (Arizona State
University), 27 (bottom left), ESA/J. Parker (Southwest Research Institute)/P. Thomas (Cornell University)/L. McFadden (University of Maryland, College Park), 17 (middle
right), ESA/M. Buie (Southwest Research Institute), 17 (top left), ESA/M. Robberto (Space Telescope Science Institute/ESA)/The Hubble Space Telescope Orion Treasury
Project Team, 24 (top left), ESA/The Hubble Heritage (STScI/AURA), 26 (bottom left), 28 (middle and bottom), 29 (bottom right), Gemini Observatory/D. Lafreniere, R.
Jayawardhana, M. van Kerkwijk (Univ. Toronto), 24 (bottom), H. Richer (University of British Columbia), 24 (top right), J. P. Harrington (U. Maryland)/K. J. Borkowski
(NCSU), 25 (top left), JPL, cover (spacecraft and Saturn), 2 (top), 14 (right), 15 (top and middle left), 18 (top left), 30 (bottom right), JPL/ESA/SSI/Cassini Imaging Team,
23 (top right), JPL/Space Science Institute, 22 (middle right), 23 (top left), JPL/UA/Lockheed Martin, 31 (middle right), JPL/University of Arizona, 14 (bottom left), JPL-
Caltech, 26 (top), NSSDC, 9 (bottom left), 23 (bottom), Robert Gendler, 29 (bottom left), SkyWorks Digital/Dana Berry, 25 (bottom), The Hubble Heritage Team (AURA/
STScI), 27 (bottom right), 28 (top right), 29 (top); Photo Researchers: Bonnier Publications/FOCI/Claus Lunau, 21 (middle right); Photodisc, back cover (top), 8 (top left), 9
(top left and right), 15 (middle right and bottom); Shutterstock: Action Sports Photography, 9 (bottom right), Alexey Filatov, 19 (middle right), alin b., 5 (bottom), Andrea
Danti, 5 (top), 8 (bottom left), 18 (bottom), andrey_l, 24 (middle right), Byron W. Moore, 16, Christos Georghiou, 5 (middle right), David P. Smith, back cover (bottom), 19
(bottom), dinadesign, 11 (middle), Dr. Ajay Kumar Singh, 13 (bottom), Dr_Flash, back cover (middle right), 9 (middle left), Elnur (torn paper), cover, 1, Igor Kovalchuk,
27 (top right), James Thew, 4 (left), Josef Muellek, 3, 19 (middle left), Konstantin Mironov, cover (middle left), 1 (left), 5
(middle left), lculig, 14 (top left), Linda Brotkorb, 4 (bottom right), Loskutnikov, 4 (top right), Marcel Clemens, 20, Mircea
Maties, 23 (middle right), Nastya Pirieva, 11 (top left), nmedia, 11 (middle right), Orla, 4 (bottom left), Paul Paladin, 10,
peresanz, 27 (top left), Shalygin, 21 (middle left), Tetyana Zhabska, 8 (right), Triff, 19 (top), Vadim Petrakov, 13 (middle
right), Viktar Malyshchyts, 26 (bottom right), Vladimir Wrangel, 13 (middle left), Walter S. Becker, 11 (bottom); SOHO
(ESA & NASA), 6, 7, 21 (bottom); Wikipedia: Gregory H. Revera, 13 (top left)

Note to Parents, Teachers, and Librarians
My First Picture Encyclopedias provide an early introduction to reference materials for young children.
These accessible, visual encyclopedias support literacy development by building subject-specific
vocabularies and research skills. Stimulating format, inviting content, and phonetic aids assist and
encourage young readers.

Printed in the United States of America in North Mankato, Minnesota.
092012   006933CGS13

Table of Contents

Amazing Space

Outer space is full of amazing things. It has giant balls of hot glowing gas and tiny, dirty, dark snowballs. An invisible force connects everything together!

star

a ball of hot, bright gas in space; our sun is a star

planet

a large round object that moves around a star; Earth is a planet

orbit

to travel around a star, planet, or any other object in space; also the path an object follows while circling another object in space

gravity

an invisible force that pulls two or more objects together; planets move around a star because gravity holds them together

moon

a small object that orbits a bigger object in space; Earth has one moon orbiting it

solar system

the sun and everything that orbits it; our solar system has eight planets and millions of smaller objects

galaxy

a very large group of stars and planets; galaxies have billions and billions of stars and planets

universe

the collection of every galaxy, star, and planet in space; the universe contains everything

Our Sun

Which star is the closest to us? It's the sun! Stars such as our sun have many layers on the inside.

core

the hot inner part of a star; the core of the sun is about 27 million degrees Fahrenheit (15 million degrees Celsius)

radiative zone

(RAY-di-ay-tiv)—the layer of the sun around the core; energy made in the sun's core moves out through the radiative zone

convection zone

(kuhn-VEK-shuhn)—the layer of the sun outside the radiative zone; the top of the convection zone is the surface of the sun

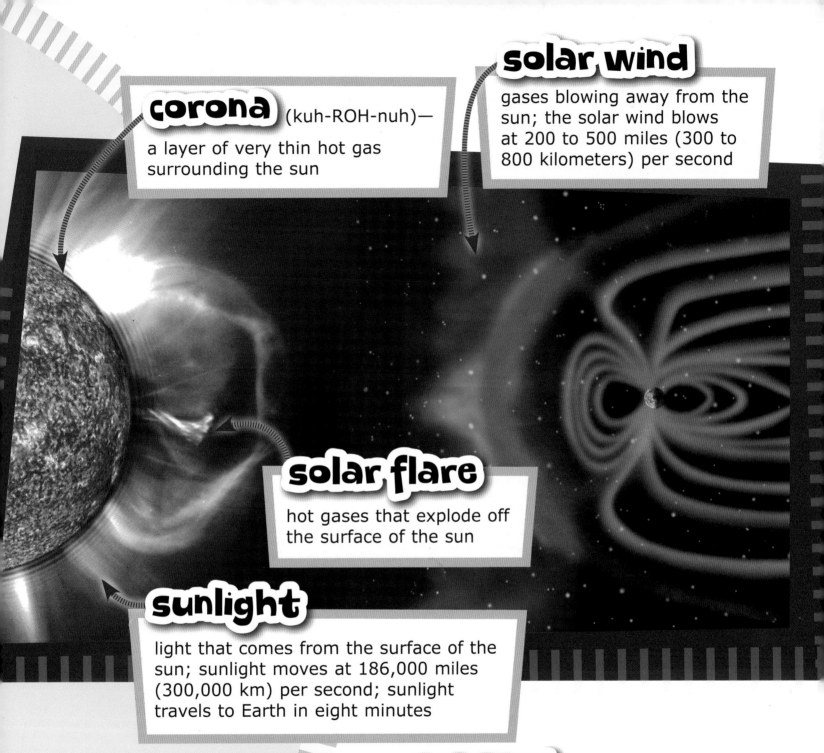

corona (kuh-ROH-nuh)—
a layer of very thin hot gas
surrounding the sun

solar wind
gases blowing away from the
sun; the solar wind blows
at 200 to 500 miles (300 to
800 kilometers) per second

solar flare
hot gases that explode off
the surface of the sun

sunlight
light that comes from the surface of the
sun; sunlight moves at 186,000 miles
(300,000 km) per second; sunlight
travels to Earth in eight minutes

sunspot
an area on the surface of the sun
that is a little cooler and gives off
less sunlight than surrounding
areas; most sunspots are
bigger than Earth

7

The Warmest Planets

Four small rocky planets orbit close to the sun. Sunlight warms their surfaces, making some of them very hot.

inner planets

the four planets in our solar system closest to the sun; each inner planet has a core made of iron and layers of rock around its core

atmosphere

a layer of gases that surrounds some planets and moons

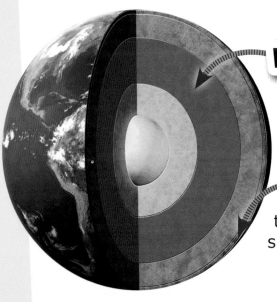

mantle

a layer around the core of a planet; inner planets have mantles made of rock

crust

the thin rocky layer on the surface of an inner planet

Mercury

smallest of the inner planets and closest to the sun; Mercury has no atmosphere

Venus

hottest of the inner planets; Venus has a very thick atmosphere that makes it warmer than Mercury; temperatures on Venus' surface reach about 850°F (450°C)

Earth

largest of the inner planets, and the planet we live on

Mars

the inner planet farthest from the sun; Mars has a thin atmosphere

volcano

a mountain that forms when hot melted rock from the mantle erupts onto the surface of a planet; the inner planets all have volcanoes; the largest volcano in the solar system is Olympus Mons on Mars

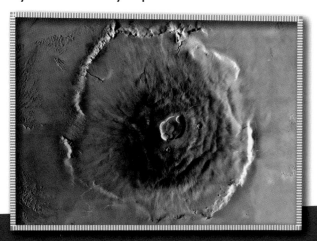

crater

a hole made when a small object from space hits a planet's surface; Mercury has the most craters of the inner planets; Earth has the fewest craters

Earth, Our Home

Earth is a beautiful blue planet. It is not too hot and not too cold.

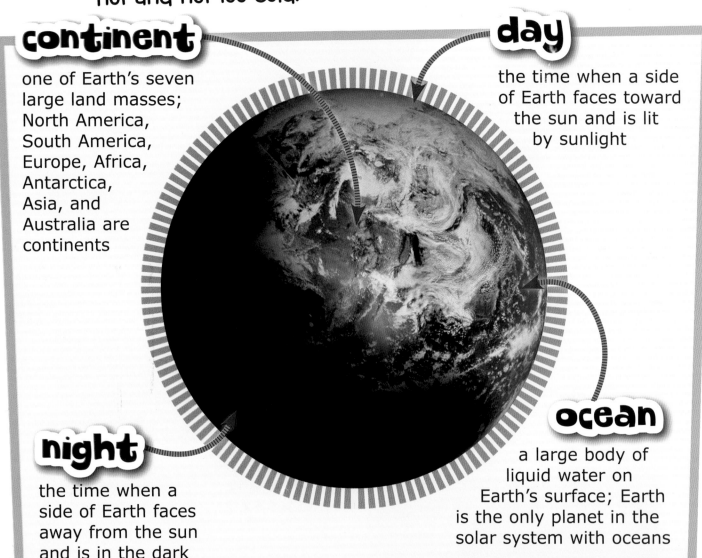

continent
one of Earth's seven large land masses; North America, South America, Europe, Africa, Antarctica, Asia, and Australia are continents

day
the time when a side of Earth faces toward the sun and is lit by sunlight

night
the time when a side of Earth faces away from the sun and is in the dark

ocean
a large body of liquid water on Earth's surface; Earth is the only planet in the solar system with oceans

microbe

life that is too small to see without a microscope; microbes can be plants, animals, or bacteria

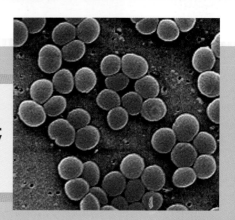

life

living things and their activity; Earth is the only planet we know of that has life

oxygen

a colorless gas that people breathe; humans and other animals need oxygen to live

photosynthesis

(foh-toh-SIN-thuh-siss)—a process that most plants and some microbes use to change sunlight into food and oxygen

aurora

(uh-ROHR-uh)—colorful bands of light in the atmosphere of Earth and other planets; aurora are caused by the solar wind and can be green, red, or yellow

Our Moon

Do you know that we can see the moon in the sky during the daytime? But no matter when we look at it, we can only see one side of the moon from Earth. It is called the near side.

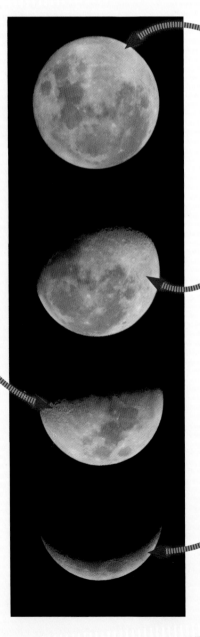

phase

the part of the moon lit up by sunlight that we can see from Earth

full moon

the phase of the moon when the entire near side is lit by sunlight

gibbous moon

the phase of the moon when more than half of the near side is lit by sunlight

quarter moon

the phase of the moon when only half of the near side is lit by sunlight; it's called quarter moon because from Earth we can see only a quarter of the entire surface of the moon

crescent moon

the phase of the moon when less than half of the near side is lit by sunlight

far side

the side of the moon that always faces away from Earth; on Earth we can never see the far side

maria

the darker areas on the moon's surface; maria formed billions of years ago when melted rock filled the bottoms of large craters; the moon's near side has many large maria, but the far side has only two tiny ones

solar eclipse

when the moon moves directly in front of the sun and its shadow falls on Earth; during a solar eclipse the sky gets as dark as at night

tides

when gravity from the moon pulls up on the water in Earth's oceans; the daily rising and falling of the ocean level

lunar eclipse

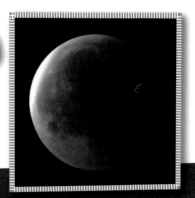

when Earth moves directly in front of the sun and its shadow falls on the moon

Giant Outer Planets

Four giant planets orbit far from the sun.
They are much bigger than the inner planets.

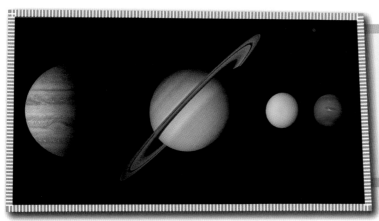

outer planets

the four giant planets in our solar system that are farthest from the sun; many moons orbit each of the four outer planets

Jupiter

a gas giant planet about 10 times larger than Earth; Jupiter is the largest planet in our solar system; if Earth were the size of a golf ball, Jupiter would be the size of a basketball; Jupiter is made mostly of hydrogen and helium gas; it has faint dusty rings and more than 60 moons

Great Red Spot

a giant storm in the clouds of Jupiter; the Great Red Spot is about twice as big as Earth

Saturn

a gas giant planet made mostly of hydrogen and helium gas; it is the second largest planet in our solar system; Saturn has bright icy rings and more than 60 moons

rings

bands of ice, rocks, and dust orbiting a planet; all four outer planets have rings around them

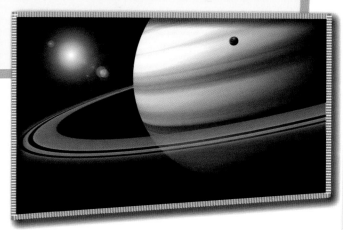

Uranus

a giant planet about four times larger than Earth; Uranus has a core of rock and iron and a mantle of water; its thick atmosphere is made of hydrogen and helium gas; Uranus has faint dusty rings and 27 known moons

Neptune

the farthest outer planet from the sun; Neptune is the coldest planet in our solar system; it has a core of rock and iron and a mantle of water; it has a thick atmosphere of hydrogen and helium gas; Neptune has faint dusty rings and 13 known moons

The Littlest Planets

Not all planets are big. Some of them are really tiny! The littlest planets are called dwarfs.

dwarf planet

a small round object orbiting the sun with many other smaller objects nearby; there are five known dwarf planets in our solar system and all are much smaller than Earth's moon

Transneptunian Object (TNO)

(transs-nep-TOON-nee-en)—an object that orbits the sun farther away than Neptune; also called a TNO; four of the dwarf planets are TNOs; more than 1,000 TNOs have been discovered

Pluto

a dwarf planet made of half ice and half rock; Pluto is a TNO with five known moons and a thin atmosphere; Pluto was discovered in 1930 and was called a planet until 2006

Eris

(AIR-is)—largest known dwarf planet and the farthest from the sun; it takes more than 550 years to orbit the sun one time; Eris was discovered in 2005 and has one known moon

Makemake

(MAH-kay MAH-kay)—a dwarf planet and TNO; Makemake takes more than 300 years to orbit the sun one time; Makemake has no known moons

Ceres

(SEER-ees)—the smallest known dwarf planet and the closest to the sun; Ceres is not a TNO because it orbits the sun between Mars and Jupiter; Ceres is made of half water and half rock; it has a mantle of water under a dusty crust

Haumea

(how-MAY-ah)— a dwarf planet and TNO with two known moons; Haumea is shaped like a football and made of solid rock

Space Rocks

Space is filled with more than just round planets.
There are also millions of lumpy, bumpy rocks.

binary asteroid

two asteroids that orbit each other; more than 100 binary asteroids are known

asteroid

a large rock in space that orbits the sun; most asteroids are made of solid rock, solid iron, or a mixture of both

meteoroids

the very smallest rocks in space that are too small for people to see from Earth; meteoroids range in size from a grain of sand to as large as a house

asteroid belt

the region between the orbits of Mars and Jupiter where most asteroids are found; more than 1 million asteroids have been discovered in the asteroid belt

meteor

the flash of light made when a meteoroid enters the atmosphere of a planet; meteors are sometimes called falling stars, but they are not stars at all

fireball

a very bright meteor made by a large meteoroid or a small asteroid

meteorite

a rock from space that lands on the surface of a planet; most meteorites are found on Earth and come from asteroids; some meteorites have been found on Mars

impact

when an asteroid or meteoroid hits a planet or another object in space; impacts of asteroids make craters

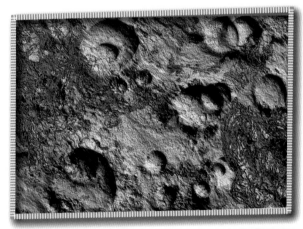

Meteor Crater

a crater in Arizona made about 50,000 years ago; the asteroid that formed Meteor Crater was traveling 26,000 miles (42,000 km) per hour when it hit Earth

Snowballs in Space

Space is the perfect place for a snowball fight! There are millions of dirty balls of ice and rock flying between the planets.

comet

a small frozen object in space with gas and dust coming off its surface; comets are made up of an icy nucleus, a coma, two tails, and a trail

nucleus

(NOO-klee-uhss)—a solid chunk of ice, rock, and dust that orbits the sun; most are less than 6 miles (10 km) across; a nucleus becomes a comet when it gets warmed by sunlight and some of the ice turns to gas

coma

a layer of gas and dust around the nucleus of a comet; a coma can be 60,000 miles (100,000 km) across

tail

a stream of dust and gas pushed away from the coma by sunlight and the solar wind; comets can have a blue gas tail and a white dust tail; comet tails can be 100 million miles (160 million km) long

Halley's Comet

the most famous comet ever seen; it has been seen by people for more than 2,000 years; Halley's Comet orbits the sun every 76 years and next comes close to Earth in 2061

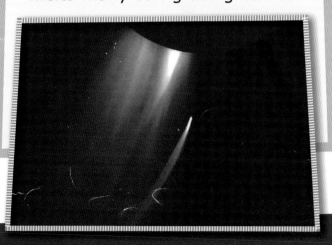

meteor shower

when hundreds or thousands of meteors happen on the same night; meteor showers occur when Earth passes through the trail of a comet and the small meteoroids enter Earth's atmosphere

sun grazing comet

a comet that gets very close to the sun; the bright sunlight close to the sun completely melts many sun grazing comets

Oort cloud

a huge, round, very cold region of the solar system that is 100,000 times farther from the sun than Earth; many comets come from the Oort cloud

Many More Moons

Our solar system has a lot of exciting moons. Some are bigger than planets! Others have erupting volcanoes! Most moons orbit asteroids instead of planets.

Io

(EYE-oh)—a moon of Jupiter with thousands of erupting volcanoes

Ganymede

(ga-NIH-meed)—the largest moon of Jupiter and the biggest moon in the solar system; Ganymede is bigger than the planet Mercury

Europa

a large icy moon of Jupiter with a deep ocean of water under a crust made of ice

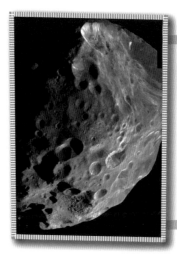

Phoebe
(FEE-bee)—a small moon of Saturn that may be a captured comet or asteroid

Titan

a large moon of Saturn with an atmosphere thicker than Earth's; Titan has lakes of liquid methane on its surface and is bigger than the planet Mercury

Charon
a large moon of Pluto; Charon is almost half the size of Pluto

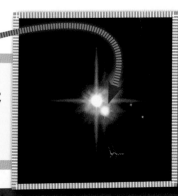

cryovolcano

(krye-oh-vol-KAY-noh)—a volcano that erupts ice or an ice-water mixture

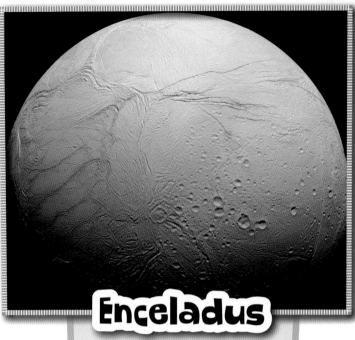

Enceladus

(en-CELL-ah-dus)—a moon of Saturn with cryovolcanoes

Triton

a large moon of Neptune with an atmosphere and cryovolcanoes

Phobos and Deimos

(FO-bos and DAY-mos)—two small moons of Mars; Phobos and Deimos may be asteroids that were held in orbit by Mars when they got too close to the planet

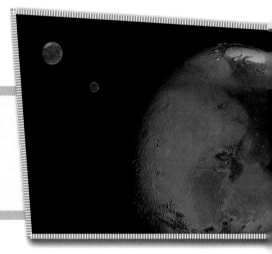

Dactyl

(DAK-tul)—a moon of the asteroid Ida; Dactyl was the first moon discovered orbiting an asteroid

The Life of a Star

Stars are born inside clouds of gas and dust. Stars come in many sizes. Most stars shine for billions of years before running out of hydrogen fuel.

molecular cloud

a huge cloud of hydrogen and helium gas; new stars form inside molecular clouds

dwarf stars

the smallest stars; it would take 10 dwarf stars put together to make our sun

red dwarf

a dwarf star that gives off mostly red light; most stars in the universe are red dwarfs

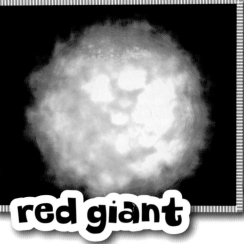

red giant

a star that has burned all the hydrogen gas in its core and has expanded to a very large size and turned red; red giants can be 100 times larger than the sun

sunlike star

a star that is about the same size as our sun

white dwarf

the hot core of a sunlike star that is left after a red giant loses most of its gas; white dwarf stars are about the size of Earth; white dwarfs have very strong gravity

supernova

the huge explosion of a star; a supernova happens to a star much bigger than our sun after it has burned all the hydrogen gas in its core

neutron star

the very tiny core of a star left behind after a supernova; neutron stars are only about 6 miles (10 km) across, about the size of a small asteroid; neutron stars have stronger gravity than white dwarfs

black hole

an area of space with gravity so strong that even light cannot escape; black holes form when the biggest stars collapse after burning all the hydrogen gas in their cores

Our Own Milky Way

A faint band of light stretches across the night sky. That band of light is our galaxy, the Milky Way. The Milky Way is crowded with about 300 billion stars.

light-year

the distance that light travels in one year; one light-year is about 6 trillion miles (10 trillion km); the Milky Way galaxy is about 100,000 light-years across

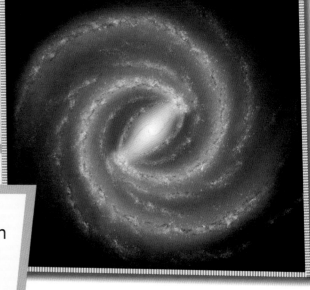

spiral galaxy

a galaxy that is flat and round, with arms in the shape of a spiral or pinwheel; the Milky Way is a spiral galaxy

star cluster

a group of stars in a galaxy that were formed together in the same molecular cloud

Pleiades

(PLEE-ah-dees)—a star cluster in the Milky Way near our sun with more than 3,000 stars

constellation

stars visible in the night sky that seem to form shapes

Orion

a constellation in the shape of a hunter

Big Dipper

a constellation in the shape of a dipper or spoon

nebula

(NEB-yuh-luh)—a huge cloud of gas and dust; some nebulae are molecular clouds and others are the leftover gas from a red giant or supernova

globular cluster

a huge round star cluster with as many as 10 million stars

Galaxies Big and Small

Our Milky Way is not alone in the universe. There are billions of other galaxies out there. They come in all shapes and sizes.

whirlpool galaxy

a spiral galaxy we see from the top that looks like a whirlpool

elliptical galaxy

(ee-LIP-tuh-kuhl)—a galaxy that has a smooth round shape; some elliptical galaxies are shaped like a football

colliding galaxies

two galaxies that are running into each other

barred galaxy

a spiral galaxy with a straight row of stars in the center; the Milky Way is a barred spiral galaxy; spiral arms come off the ends of the bar

Sombrero Galaxy

(sohm-BRER-oh)—a spiral galaxy we see from the side that looks like a high-crowned hat called a sombrero

satellite galaxy

a small galaxy that orbits a much bigger galaxy

Antennae Galaxies

(an-TEH-nee)—colliding galaxies that look like antennae on a bug

Seyfert Galaxy

(SEE-furt)—a spiral galaxy with a huge black hole in the center

Magellanic Clouds

(mah-ja-LAH-nik)—two tiny dwarf galaxies that are satellite galaxies of the Milky Way

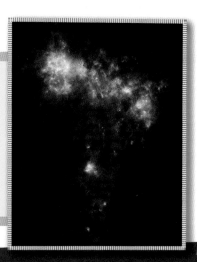

Studying Space

Do you want to study space? Scientists use a lot of tools to explore things in our solar system and beyond.

astronomer

a scientist who studies galaxies, stars, planets, and other objects in space

Hubble Space Telescope

a telescope put into space so that it would be above the clouds in Earth's atmosphere

telescope

a tool used by astronomers to look at objects in space; telescopes make distant objects appear bigger and brighter

spacecraft

a vehicle that travels in space using rockets; most spacecraft do not carry people

mission

the effort by a team of scientists to explore objects in space using spacecraft, landers, or rovers

rover

a vehicle that scientists drive using remote control; rovers move around on an object after landing

lander

a vehicle that lands on the surface of an object to study it

Mars Exploration Rovers

a mission using twin rovers to explore the surface of Mars; the rovers are named *Spirit* and *Opportunity*

Phoenix

(FEE-nix)—a mission that landed near the north pole of Mars and discovered ice under the dirt

Rosetta

a mission to study a comet with a spacecraft and a lander

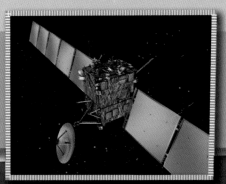

Mars Science Laboratory

a mission exploring the surface and atmosphere of Mars using a giant rover named *Curiosity*

Read More

Conrad, David. *Exploring Space*. Earth and Space Science. Mankato, Minn.: Capstone Press, 2012.

Hughes, Catherine D. *First Big Book of Space*. National Geographic Little Kids. Washington, D.C.: National Geographic, 2012.

Peters, Elisa. *Outer Space*. The Universe. New York: PowerKids Press, 2013.

Titles in this set:

Show me
COMMUNITY HELPERS

Show me
DINOSAURS

Show me
DOGS

Show me
INSECTS

Show me
POLAR ANIMALS

Show me
REPTILES

Show me
SPACE

Show me
TRANSPORTATION

Internet Sites

FactHound offers a safe, fun way to find Internet sites related to this book. All of the sites on FactHound have been researched by our staff.

Here's all you do:

Visit *www.facthound.com*

Type in this code: 9781620650585

Super-cool stuff!

Check out projects, games and lots more at
www.capstonekids.com